GRETA THUNBERG

GRETA THUNBERG

Climate Crisis Activist

MATT DOEDEN

LERNER PUBLICATIONS ◆ MINNEAPOLIS

Lerner Publications Company
An imprint of Lerner Publishing Group, Inc.
241 First Avenue North
Minneapolis, MN 55401 USA

For reading levels and more information, look up this title at www.lernerbooks.com.

Image credits: MICHAEL CAMPANELLA/Getty Images, pp. 2, 8; Marc Piscotty/Getty Images, p. 6; HENRIK MONTGOMERY/TT News Agency/AFP/Getty Images, p. 10; lexaarts/Shutterstock .com, p. 11; Amani A/Shutterstock.com, p. 12; jo Crebbin/Shutterstock.com, p. 13; MALIN HOELSTAD/SVD/TT/TT NEWS AGENCY/AFP/Getty Images, p. 15; JANEK SKARZYNSKI/ AFP/Getty Images, p. 16; RHONA WISE/AFP/Getty Images, p. 17; HANNA FRANZEN/AFP/ Getty Images, p. 18; Peter Kneffel/picture alliance/Getty Images, p. 19; Guido Kirchner/picture alliance/Getty Images, p. 20; Beata Zawrzel/NurPhoto/Getty Images, p. 21; SUMY SADURNI/ AFP/Getty Images, p. 22; Michele Crowe/CBS/Getty Images, p. 23; Paramonov Alexander/ Shutterstock.com, p. 24; Win McNamee/Getty Images, p. 25; LIONEL BONAVENTURE/AFP/Getty Images, p. 26; TIMOTHY A. CLARY/AFP/Getty Images, p. 28; AndriiKoval/Shutterstock .com, p. 29; Horacio Villalobos/Getty Images, p. 31; Pablo Blazquez Dominguez/Getty Images, p. 32; franz12/Shutterstock.com, p. 34; Per Grunditz/Shutterstock.com, p. 35; Ronald Patrick/ Getty Images, p. 36; FABRICE COFFRINI/AFP/Getty Images, p. 37; andyparker72/Shutterstock .com, p. 38; 1000 Words/Shutterstock.com, p. 39. Cover image: Michael Campanella/Getty Images.

Main body text set in Rotis Serif Std. Typeface provided by Monotype Typography.

Editor: Shee Yang **Designer:** Lauren Cooper
Lerner team: Sue Marquis

Library of Congress Cataloging-in-Publication Data

Names: Doeden, Matt, author.
Title: Greta thunberg : climate crisis activist / Matt Doeden.
Description: Minneapolis, MN : Lerner Publications , 2021. | Series: Gateway biographies | Includes bibliographical references and index. | Audience: Ages 9–14 | Audience: Grades 4–6 | Summary: "Motivated by government apathy regarding climate change, 15-year-old Greta Thunberg held a demonstration that would ignite a global movement. Read more about Greta and the environmental movement that is changing the world"– Provided by publisher.
Identifiers: LCCN 2020005548 (print) | LCCN 2020005549 (ebook) | ISBN 9781541596795 (library binding) | ISBN 9781728400303 (ebook other)
Subjects: LCSH: Thunberg, Greta, 2003–Juvenile literature. | Child environmentalists–Sweden– Biography–Juvenile literature. | Environmentalists–Sweden–Biography–Juvenile literature.
Classification: LCC GE56.T58 D64 2021 (print) | LCC GE56.T58 (ebook) | DDC 363.70092 [B]– dc23

LC record available at https://lccn.loc.gov/2020005548
LC ebook record available at https://lccn.loc.gov/2020005549

Manufactured in the United States of America
4-52282-48226-6/1/2023

CONTENTS

Greta Thunberg speaks in Denver, Colorado, during a climate strike on October 11, 2019.

On August 20, 2018, fifteen-year-old Greta Thunberg stood alone outside of the Parliament House in Stockholm, Sweden. Greta had just started the ninth grade and was expected to be in school. She had come here instead to voice her deep concerns about climate change and the terrible consequences it would have if people don't change how they generate and use energy.

Greta had long been worried about how the burning of fossil fuels was impacting Earth's climate. For years she had been fixated on the crisis. She'd done all she could to reduce her own energy use. But Greta knew she couldn't do it alone. She often felt depressed, believing that she did not have the power or influence to combat what she considered the biggest crisis in human history. So when she saw student-organized protests against gun violence in the United States, she vowed to go on a school strike until the Swedish elections were held in early September.

On that first day, Greta quietly passed out fliers that described the dangers of climate change. She held a handmade sign that read *Skolstrejk för klimatet*, Swedish for "School strike for climate." Greta talked to anyone willing to listen. And she did it all alone. Despite her efforts to get other students to join her, none had. She felt that she needed to take a stand, even if she was alone in doing so.

"I painted the sign on a piece of wood and, for the fliers, wrote down some facts I thought everyone should know," Greta explained. "And then I took my bike to the parliament and just sat there. The first day, I sat alone from about 8:30 a.m. to 3:00 p.m.—the regular school day."

Greta poses for a photo during a school strike outside of the Swedish parliament on August 28, 2018.

It was a small gesture that could easily have gone unnoticed. But it didn't. Before her strike, Greta had posted her plans to social media. Word spread, and soon local reporters joined her in front of the Parliament House to cover her strike. "On the second day, people started joining me," she recalled. "After that, there were people there all the time."

As word spread, support for Greta's strike grew. By September, after the elections, Greta was leading strikes every Friday. More and more students joined her, and the world noticed. Greta was making international news, sparking discussion, creating awareness, and reminding people of all ages that it is the children who bear the burden of the worst effects of climate change.

With nothing but a sign and some fliers, a teenager had sparked one of the biggest climate movements. And she was just getting started.

Born in Sweden

Greta Tintin Eleonora Ernman Thunberg was born on January 3, 2003, in Stockholm, Sweden. Her mother, Malena Ernman, was a famous opera singer. Her father, Svante Thunberg, was an actor. In 2006, the family welcomed another girl, Beata. Thunberg took a break from his acting career to care for the girls, while Ernman continued to tour the world.

Greta (*right*) and her sister Beata Thunberg (*left*) march for climate change awareness in Stockholm, Sweden, on March 15, 2019.

When Greta was eleven years old, she and her little sister were diagnosed with Asperger's syndrome, also known as autism spectrum disorder (ASD). ASD doesn't affect someone's ability to learn or think, but it makes it harder to interact with others.

When something interested Greta, her focus was razor-sharp and her curiosity took over. "My brain works a bit different," Greta later explained. "And I usually don't enjoy participating in the social game that [others] seem so fond of. And I don't like lying. And I see things black or white." Greta's conviction and focus pushed her to learn all she could about climate change.

Greta was about eight years old when she first learned about climate change. She didn't entirely believe it at first. "I remember thinking that it was very strange that humans, who are an animal species among others, could be capable of changing the earth's climate," she said. "Because, if we were and if it was really happening, we wouldn't be talking about anything else. As soon as you turned on the TV, everything would be about that. . . . But no one talked about it." Her disbelief pushed her to learn more about the causes and consequences of climate change. Greta began recognizing the indifference

Air pollution is responsible for about 9 percent of deaths worldwide.

A student holds up a sign during a demonstration on September 20, 2019.

around climate change, especially among community and world leaders who she believes have the responsibility to educate and protect the public. Greta observed the habits of everyday people. She deemed their routines wasteful and careless. Greta also began to question the lack of public awareness due to the silence and greed of those making a profit off of spoiling Earth. She began to feel small and wondered why people seemed to care as little for Earth as they did one another.

The more Greta learned, the more desperate the situation seemed to become. Everything was wrong to Greta. The world felt as damaged as the people living in it. She knew she couldn't accept what was happening, but she was trapped. What could a child do to protect her future, especially when she felt she was the only one who recognized how dire the situation was. Greta began to retreat. "She could not cope with [it]," said her father. "So, she fell into a depression. She stopped eating, stopped talking."

Greta was deeply affected by what was happening. Other kids her age worried about it too, but they didn't seem to dwell on it the way she did. "I overthink," she explained. "Some people can just let things go, but I can't, especially if there's something that worries me or makes me sad. I remember when I was younger, and in school, our teachers showed us films of plastic in the ocean, starving polar bears and so on. I cried through all the movies. My classmates were concerned when they watched the film, but when it stopped, they started thinking about other things. I couldn't do that. Those pictures were stuck in my head."

Arctic ice has decreased in thickness by 40 percent since the 1960s, causing elevated sea levels and loss of habitat for many animals.

What Is Climate Change?

Climate change, or global warming, is one of the biggest challenges facing the human race. Climate change refers to the changes to Earth's atmosphere that are caused by human activities.

The most common way of creating energy is by burning fossil fuels. Fossil fuels contain hundreds of millions of years' worth of carbon buildup from prehistoric plants and animals. Burning these fuels releases carbon dioxide, or CO_2.

This gas helps to trap the heat generated by sunlight in Earth's atmosphere. As more and more CO_2 is released into the air, more heat becomes trapped in the atmosphere. Global temperatures rise, and weather patterns change. These changes threaten entire ecosystems.

Change and Despair

Greta tried to make changes at home. She pushed her family to use less energy and reduce their carbon footprint, or how much CO_2 a person or group puts into the atmosphere. She vowed to stop flying in airplanes since they use massive amounts of fuel. She convinced her parents to stop flying. Then Greta learned about the production of meat and its devastating contribution to the emission of greenhouse gases, such as CO_2. So she gave up meat and dairy products.

Next, she tried to convince her parents to do the same. She presented charts and graphs that showed how harmful meat production is to the environment. That didn't work. But Greta doesn't give up so easily and came up with a new approach: she made it personal. She told

her parents that they were stealing her future by eating meat. After that, the Thunberg family became vegan. "I realized that she was right and I was wrong, and I had been wrong all my life," her father said.

In her home, Greta was able to confront climate change, but she understood that changing the course of the future would require much more. She knew that change would only come when the measures taken to prevent and perhaps even reverse the worst effects of the crisis were as big as the crisis itself.

Greta's depression deepened. She stopped talking. She wouldn't eat. At times she wouldn't go to school. "Nothing really was happening in my life," she said. "I have always been that girl in the back who doesn't say anything. I thought I couldn't make a difference because I was too small."

In February 2018, a tragic event left the world stunned. A young man armed with assault weapons entered Marjory Stoneman Douglas High School in Parkland, Florida. The shooter opened fire, killing seventeen people and injuring seventeen more. The tragedy marked the beginning of a wave of anti-gun protests from students in Parkland and around the world. For a moment, it seemed as if the world was tuned in. "What if children did that for the climate?" she asked a friend. The seed had been planted. She felt that climate change was the most important problem the world faced, and the children who marched against guns inspired her. They wanted their futures just as much as she wanted hers, and they were changing public opinion.

"I decided enough was enough," she later wrote. "Sweden had just experienced its hottest summer ever. The election was coming up. No one was talking about climate change as an actual consequence of our way of life. . . . Because if climate change has to stop, then we must stop it. It is black and white. There are no gray areas when it comes to survival. Either we continue as a civilization or we don't. One way or another, we have to change."

Protesters hold up signs outside of the Broward County Federal Courthouse in Fort Lauderdale, Florida, on February 17, 2018, after the school shooting in Parkland.

In May 2018, Greta wrote an essay about climate change that was published by a Swedish newspaper. Greta's movement had begun. Swedish environmentalists began contacting her to talk about climate change, what's at stake for children, and what children can do to help support her cause. Greta took the opportunity to suggest organizing school strikes, just as the US anti-gun students had done.

Greta's parents tried to talk her out of it. Her teachers offered her different ideas for how she could protest,

Greta holds a sign that means "school strike for the climate" outside of Sweden's Parliament House on November 30, 2018.

without missing so much school. None of them could change her mind. She had a plan, and she was going to carry it out.

On August 20, 2018, Greta rode her bike to the Parliament House in Stockholm. She was supposed to go to school that day. But she didn't. Greta posted about her strike on social media and tried to get other young people to join her, but no one did. So she went by herself. The fifteen-year-old stood alone in silent protest, hoping someone would notice.

And they did. Within a week, others were joining her. Dozens grew to hundreds. Hundreds grew to thousands. The young teen was quickly becoming the face of the fight against climate change.

Empowered by the support of her peers, Greta was even more focused and determined. Like the anti-gun student protests, Greta's climate movement was being noticed around the world. She poured all of her energy into combating the climate crisis. And the weight of feeling powerless lifted. "Learning about climate change triggered my depression in the first place," she said. "But it was also what got me out of my depression, because there were things I could do to improve the situation. I don't have time to be depressed anymore."

Following Greta's lead, students in Munich, Germany, hold a demonstration against climate change on January 18, 2019.

Building the Movement

What began as a single person silently protesting suddenly became a worldwide conversation. People of all ages who were worried about climate change rallied alongside Greta. Climate change awareness skyrocketed. Greta found hope in learning that she was not the only person who wanted a different future than the one the world was headed toward.

After the Swedish elections in September 2018, Greta began leading strikes every Friday. She called the strikes the Fridays for Future campaign. Soon students all around the world were staging their own strikes. By November more than seventeen thousand students spread across twenty-four countries took part in the walkouts.

A farmer in Germany turns his cornfield into a protest sign in support of Greta and the movement against climate change.

As support continued to grow and news coverage broadened, Greta's environmental knowledge, passion, and manner of speaking propelled her into the spotlight even further.

On December 12, 2018, Greta was invited to speak at the United Nations (UN) Climate Conference (COP24) in Poland. Nations around the world sent representatives to the summit to discuss the problem and develop solutions.

Greta at COP24 in Poland

But Greta was not impressed. She needed world leaders to commit to more and focus on the value of life.

"You are not mature enough to tell it like [it] is," she said. "Even that burden you leave to us children. But I don't care about being popular. I care about climate justice and the living planet. Our civilization is being sacrificed for the opportunity of a very small number of people to continue making enormous amounts of money. Our biosphere is being sacrificed so that rich people in countries like mine can live in luxury. It is the sufferings of the many which pay for the luxuries of the few. . . .

"The year 2078, I will celebrate my 75th birthday," she continued. "If I have children maybe they will spend that day with me. Maybe they will ask me about you. Maybe they will ask why you didn't do anything while there still was time to act. You say you love your children above all else, and yet you are stealing their future in front of their very eyes. Until you start focusing on what needs to be done rather than what is politically possible, there is no hope. We can't solve a crisis without treating it as a crisis."

Inspired by Greta, fifteen-year-old Leah Namugera carries a sign around Kampala, Uganda, to raise awareness about global warming.

By March more than two million people in 135 countries had taken part in school strikes against climate change, including strikes in Uganda,

Bangladesh, and Indonesia. Reporters wanted to interview Greta. TV shows invited her to talk about the movement. She had become an international icon. But Greta stayed grounded. She continued going to school, even when her hectic schedule made it a challenge.

Greta sits down for an early morning interview on *CBS This Morning.*

Praise and Criticism

Greta's rapid rise to the world stage earned her plenty of praise. In December 2018, *Time* magazine included her on its list of the 25 most influential teenagers in the world. Four months later, *Time* listed her among the 100 most influential people in the world. In March 2019, Greta was nominated for the Nobel Peace Prize for her environmental work.

The Nobel Prize is awarded to people who have done outstanding work in the fields of physics, chemistry, medicine or physiology, literature, peace, or economics.

Although Greta was glad for the attention her strike brought to climate change, she didn't always welcome everything else that came with it. In November 2018, she was nominated for the Children's Climate Prize in Sweden. Despite feeling grateful, she declined the nomination. She explained that many of the finalists for the award would have to fly to the ceremony in Stockholm and that it was needlessly wasteful. Greta discouraged and avoided flying as often as she could. Flying was a major contributor to greenhouse gases. She traveled mostly by train across

Europe and beyond to deliver speeches about global warming and leading greener and cleaner lifestyles. Greta stood her ground, practicing what she preached, and nothing could steer her away from her cause.

But not everyone was pleased with Greta or what she represented. Climate change deniers opposed Greta and her message passionately. Many individuals and businesses felt threatened by her message. Some claimed that global warming was a natural phenomenon. They believed people had nothing to do with Earth's temperature rising. Others criticized her approach. They believed that despite humans being responsible for the

Then Environmental Protection Agency administrator Scott Pruitt (*right*) addresses Donald Trump's (*left*) decision to pull the US out of the Paris Agreement, which requires the countries involved to reduce their carbon footprint and prevent more climate change.

increased rate of global warming, Greta's solutions to the crisis were childish and unrealistic. But above all else, they believed what Greta was asking of the world was too much of a cost to pay.

Greta delivers a speech at the French Parliament on July 23, 2019.

ASSEMBLÉE NATIONALE
semblee-nat

Mardi 23 juillet 2019

In July 2019, Greta spoke at the French Parliament. Her appearance didn't make everyone happy. Many politicians called for a boycott of her speech. Greta replied by telling them that they didn't have to listen to her. But they did have to listen to the science.

The Tipping Point

Much of Greta's message centers on the tipping point of climate change. The tipping point is the point at which climate change will become more abrupt and irreversible. Not everyone agrees on what the tipping point might be. But most climate scientists think that it might be an average global temperature rise of 2.7°F to 3.6°F (1.5°C to 2°C). And some believe we may have already reached the tipping point.

According to climate scientists, if the atmosphere reaches the tipping point, it could cause a catastrophic global warming cycle beyond repair. Greta's movement is focused on ways to avoid this disaster.

Making Waves

Greta traveled to New York City to speak at the UN Climate Action Summit. But as a climate-conscious traveler, she refused to fly. Instead, Greta hitched a ride on a solar-powered sailboat. It was a fifteen-day journey. Once in the US, Greta's first stop was Capitol Hill, where she spoke to Congress about climate change and what the US can do to help.

On September 23, a little more than a year after she began her strike against climate change, Greta addressed world leaders once more. At the UN Climate Action Summit in New York City, the sixteen-year-old would deliver one of her most powerful statements to date.

"I shouldn't be up here," she said. "I should be back in school on the other side of the ocean. Yet you all come to us young people for hope. How dare you! You have stolen my dreams and my childhood with your empty words. And yet I'm one of the lucky ones. People are suffering. People are dying. Entire ecosystems are collapsing. We are in the beginning of a mass extinction, and all you can talk about is money and fairy tales of eternal economic growth. How dare you!

"You are failing us," she concluded. "But the young people are starting to understand your betrayal. The eyes of all future generations are upon you. And if you choose to fail us, I say: We will never forgive you. We will not let you get away with this. Right here, right now is where we draw the line. The world is waking up. And change is coming, whether you like it or not."

Greta delivers her most famous speech at the 2019 UN Climate Action Summit.

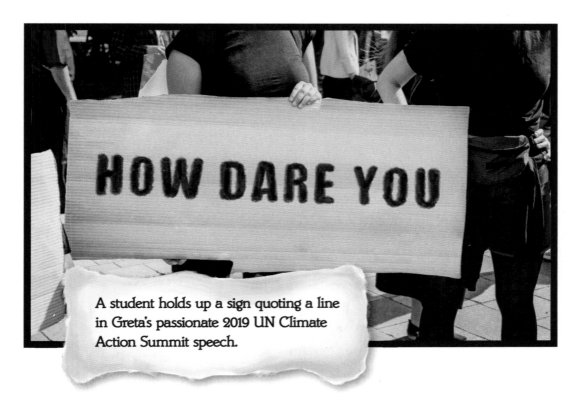

A student holds up a sign quoting a line in Greta's passionate 2019 UN Climate Action Summit speech.

People at the highest levels of power were listening—even if they didn't like the message. The day after her speech, US president Donald Trump responded to Greta on Twitter. Trump, who has largely denied that climate change is a problem, appeared to mock the sixteen-year-old for her passion. "She seems like a very happy young girl looking forward to a bright and wonderful future. So nice to see!"

Former vice president Joe Biden was quick to come to Greta's defense. "What kind of president bullies a teenager?" he wrote. "[Donald Trump], you could learn a few things from Greta on what it means to be a leader."

Return to Europe

Greta had planned to travel south to Chile for the UN's Climate Change Conference (COP25) in December 2019. But a growing public unrest in Chile forced the conference to be moved to Madrid, Spain. Greta wanted to be there, but she refused to fly.

She turned to social media for a solution. "As COP25 has officially been moved from Santiago to Madrid I'll need some help," she tweeted. "Now I need to find a way to cross the Atlantic in November. . . . If anyone could help me find transport, I would be so grateful."

She didn't have to wait long. An Australian family sailing around the world offered her a ride. So on November 13, Greta and her father joined the family on their boat, *La Vagabonde*, and headed for Europe. Greta quickly bonded with her shipmates, Elayna Carausu, Riley Whitelum, and their young son, Lenny, who she took care of while his parents sailed the ship.

"Before we left with all the media she was like in her own little world and then as soon as we got on the boat and left she was overwhelmed with what had just happened," said Carausu. "But within a few days she was at ease and doing her exercises, listening to her audiobook, helping me with the cooking and she just seemed really relaxed, you could tell."

Greta (*front*) stands with the mayor of Lisbon (*right*), sailboat owners Carausu and Whitelum, and yachtswoman Nicola Henderson after embarking on the trip from America back to Europe to attend COP25.

Greta said that she was eager to get back home and that she was looking forward to reuniting with her two dogs, Moses and Roxy. "I really miss having a routine because now I've been on the road constantly for several months," she explained. "I like routines, so it would be nice to get those routines back."

La Vagabonde arrived at a port in Lisbon, Portugal, on December 3. She was greeted by supporters, including professional yachtswoman Nicola Henderson and the mayor of Lisbon. From Lisbon, Greta traveled by train to Madrid, just in time to make the conference, which ran

Greta speaks at COP25 on December 11, 2019, in Madrid, Spain.

from December 2 to 13. Huge crowds gathered around her as she arrived. It wasn't attention she wanted, but she had a sense of humor about it. She posted a video of reporters mobbing her and added the message, "I successfully managed to sneak into Madrid this morning! I don't think anyone saw me. . . ."

At the conference, Greta's speech took on a different tone. Her usual anger was replaced by frustration and a desperate appeal for action. "We have been striking for over a year, and basically nothing has happened," she said. "The climate crisis is still being ignored by those in power, and we cannot go on like this."

Big Problems, Big Solutions

The question of how to combat climate change is a big one, and not everyone agrees on the answers. But many experts believe that two broad categories of change must be made: mitigation and adaptation.

Adaptation is about learning to adjust to climate changes that have already been set in motion. It's an important and necessary step, but it's focused on reacting to change, not preventing further damage.

Mitigation is about reducing the amount of harmful gases such as CO_2 that humans put into the atmosphere. This is the focus of Greta's message. Mitigation means serious reductions in the mining and use of fossil fuels and increasing the use of clean energy sources, including solar, wind, and nuclear power. It may also mean a global shift toward plant-based diets, to reduce CO_2 emissions. According to many climate scientists, these changes need to happen within the next decade or so to avoid many of the worst effects of climate change.

Person of the Year

Greta kept making headlines, to the delight of her fans and followers. Perhaps her biggest headline yet came on December 4, 2019. At the end of every year, *Time* magazine releases an issue centered on a person who they feel has made a big impact in the previous year. Winners have included presidents, world and religious leaders, business leaders, and scientists. For 2019 *Time* chose Greta. The cover of the magazine featured her standing on the coast of Lisbon, Portugal, with the headline: "Greta Thunberg: The Power of Youth."

Greta on the cover
of *Time* magazine's
December 2019 issue

The article described Greta's unique personality as the driving force behind the growing movement. "She dislikes crowds; ignores small talk; and speaks in direct, uncomplicated sentences," the authors wrote. "She cannot be flattered or distracted. She is not impressed by other people's celebrity, nor does she seem to have interest in her own growing fame. But these very qualities have helped make her a global sensation. Where others smile to cut the tension, Thunberg is withering. Where others speak the language of hope, Thunberg repeats the unassailable science: Oceans will rise. Cities will flood. Millions of people will suffer."

Time's selection of Greta didn't go unnoticed by her opponents, including Trump, who may have been hoping to earn the honor for himself. He took the conversation to Twitter in an unprompted response. Just as he had in August, Trump mocked Greta for her passion and her cause. "So ridiculous," he tweeted. "Greta must work on her Anger Management problem, then go to a good old fashioned movie with a friend! Chill Greta, Chill!"

Even as others came to her defense, calling out Trump for bullying a sixteen-year-old, Greta took the criticism with humor. She quickly responded by altering her own Twitter profile to read, "A teenager working on her anger management problem. Currently chilling and watching a good old-fashioned movie with a friend."

Greta on her seventeenth birthday on January 3, 2020

Greta Persists

Greta charged into 2020 with the same determination she'd shown since bursting onto the scene less than two years before. In January she spoke at the World Economic

Greta poses with student climate activists on January 17, 2020, in Lausanne, Switzerland.

Forum's annual meeting, in Davos, Switzerland. She was part of a march, held largely by young people, designed to pressure world leaders into making reasonable changes that would stop governments from supporting fossil fuels. Greta and others took to the streets, carrying signs and demanding change.

Greta spoke to economic leaders, telling them that they were failing and that their policies were dooming civilization as they know it. "We must change almost everything in our current societies," she said. "The bigger your carbon footprint, the bigger your moral duty. The bigger your platform, the bigger your responsibility. Adults keep saying: 'We owe it to the young people to give them hope.' But I don't want your hope. I don't want you to be hopeful. I want you to panic. I want you to feel the fear I feel every day. And then I want you to act. I want you to act as you would in a crisis. I want you to act as if our house is on fire. Because it is."

As usual, not everyone was open to her opinion. US secretary of the treasury Steven Mnuchin replied, "Is she the chief economist? Who is she? I'm confused. . . . After she goes and studies economics in college, she can go back and explain that to us."

Greta walks past King Phillippe of Belgium during the annual World Economic Forum.

Protesters carry a sign with Greta's likeness during the Bristol Youth Strike 4 Climate event in England on February 27, 2020.

Greta responded to Mnuchin's criticism in typical fashion, tweeting, "It doesn't take a college degree in economics to realize that our remaining 1.5° [2.7°F] carbon budget and ongoing fossil fuel subsidies and investments don't add up."

With the facts on her side, Greta didn't back down in the face of criticism, even from people at the highest levels of power. She knew that she was right. And more than that, she knew it was her future and the future of children everywhere that she was fighting for.

In a year and a half, Greta's lone protest turned into a global movement. Climate change awareness has increased substantially, from the way it is handled by politicians to the way everyday people think about one-time-use plastics such as straws and disposable utensils. Greta has brought this crisis to the forefront, as well as the awareness that the decisions made by a few in the past and present have selfishly compromised the future for everyone, especially children.

When asked if she would still be doing this work in five years, Greta said, "I think that I will be doing . . . something," she said. "I won't be as interesting in people's eyes, of course, as I am now. That will fade away eventually. But I will still try to do everything I can from where I am."

Greta stands with student protesters at the Bristol Youth Strike 4 Climate event.

IMPORTANT DATES

2003	Greta Thunberg is born on January 3 in Stockholm, Sweden.
2011	Greta first becomes concerned about climate change and cannot understand why people aren't doing more to combat it.
2014	Greta is diagnosed with autism spectrum disorder.
February 2018	A school shooting in Florida sets off a wave of student protests that inspire Greta's school strike.
May 2018	A Swedish newspaper publishes an essay written by Greta on the dangers of climate change.
August 2018	On August 20, Greta begins her school strike.
September 2018	Greta begins her Fridays for Future campaign, encouraging students to strike from school on Fridays to demand action on climate change.

December 2018	Greta speaks about climate change at a COP24.
	Time magazine names her one of the 25 most influential teenagers in the world.
September 2019	Greta speaks at the UN Climate Action Summit in New York City.
November 2019	Greta sails back to Europe to attend the upcoming COP25.
December 2019	Greta speaks at COP25.
	Greta is named *Time*'s Person of the Year.
January 2020	At the World Economic Forum in Davos, Switzerland, Greta urges economists to steer away from fossil fuels.
	Greta is nominated for a Nobel Peace Prize for the second year in a row.

SOURCE NOTES

8   Jonathan Watts, "Greta Thunberg, Schoolgirl Climate Change Warrior: 'Some People Can Let Things Go. I Can't,'" *Guardian* (US edition), March 11, 2019, https://www.theguardian.com /world/2019/mar/11/greta-thunberg-schoolgirl-climate-change -warrior-some-people-can-let-things-go-i-cant.

9   Watts.

10   "School Strike for Climate: Meet 15-Year-Old Activist Greta Thunberg, Who Inspired a Global Movement," *Democracy Now!*, December 11, 2018, https://www.democracynow.org/2018/12/11 /meet_the_15_year_old_swedish.

11   Greta Thunberg, "School Strike for Climate—Save the World by Changing the Rules," TED, accessed March 30, 2020, https:// www.ted.com/talks/greta_thunberg_school_strike_for_climate _save_the_world_by_changing_the_rules/transcript?language=en.

12–13   "School Strike for Climate," *Democracy Now!*

13   Watts, "Greta Thunberg."

15   Charlotte Alter, Suyin Haynes, and Justin Worland, "*Time* 2019 Person of the Year: Greta Thunberg," *Time*, December 4, 2019, https://time.com/person-of-the-year-2019-greta-thunberg/.

15   Watts, "Greta Thunberg."

16   "School Strike for Climate," *Democracy Now!*

17   Greta Thunberg, "I'm Striking from School to Protest Inaction on Climate Change—You Should Too," *Guardian* (US edition), November 26, 2018, https://www.theguardian.com /commentisfree/2018/nov/26/im-striking-from-school-for -climate-change-too-save-the-world-australians-students -should-too.

19   Alter, Haynes, and Worland, "*Time* 2019 Person of the Year."

21–22   Greta Thunberg, in Emanuele Rigitano, "COP24, the Speech by 15-Year-Old Climate Activist Greta Thunberg Everyone Should Listen To," transcript, LifeGate, December 17, 2018, https://www .lifegate.com/people/news/greta-thunberg-speech-cop24.

22   Thunberg.

27–28   "Transcript: Greta Thunberg's Speech at the U.N. Climate Action Summit," NPR, September 23, 2019, https://www.npr.org /2019/09/23/763452863/transcript-greta-thunbergs-speech -at-the-u-n-climate-action-summit.

28   "Transcript."

29   Veronica Stracqualursi, "Trump Again Mocks Teen Climate Activist Greta Thunberg," CNN, December 12, 2019, https://www .cnn.com/2019/12/12/politics/trump-greta-thunberg-time-person -of-the-year/index.html.

29   Stracqualursi.

30   Rhiannon Shine and James Carmody, "Greta Thunberg Catches Lift to UN COP25 Climate Summit in Madrid with Australian Sailing Couple," ABC.net.au, November 13, 2019, https://www.abc.net.au/news/2019-11-13/australian-sailors-taking-greta-thunberg-back-to-un-cop25-summit/11699990.

30   Briana Shepherd, "Greta Thunberg's *La Vagabonde* Voyage Let an Aussie Family Meet the Girl behind a Climate Movement," ABC.net.au, December 5, 2019, https://www.abc.net.au/news/2019-12-05/the-real-greta-thunberg-emerged-aboard-la-vagabonde/11766208.

31   Emily Holden, "Greta Thunberg Leaves US with Simple Climate Crisis Message: Vote," *Guardian* (US edition), November 12, 2019, https://www.theguardian.com/environment/2019/nov/12/greta-thunberg-climate-crisis-message-vote.

32   Emanuela Barbiroglio, "COP25: Greta Thunberg Arrives in Madrid," *Forbes*, December 6, 2019, https://www.forbes.com/sites/emanuelabarbiroglio/2019/12/06/cop25-greta-thunberg-arrives-in-madrid/#5739876d7560.

32   Bianca Britton, "Greta Thunberg Criticizes World Leaders' Climate Actions as They Meet at COP25 to Discuss the Crisis," CNN.com, December 6, 2019, https://www.cnn.com/2019/12/06/europe/greta-thunberg-cop25-climate-crisis-intl/index.html.

32   Andrea Germanos, "Even as 500,000 March in Madrid, Greta Thunberg Warns Climate Movement Has 'Achieved Nothing' Until Emissions Fall," Common Dreams, December 6, 2019, https://www.commondreams.org/news/2019/12/06/even-500000-march-madrid-greta-thunberg-warns-climate-movement-has-achieved-nothing.

34   Alter, Haynes, and Worland, "*Time* 2019 Person of the Year."

35   "Trump Mocks Teen Climate Activist Thunberg: 'Chill Greta, Chill,'" Reuters, December 12, 2019, https://www.reuters.com/article/us-usa-trump-gretathunberg/trump-mocks-teen-climate-activist-thunberg-chill-greta-chill-idUSKBN1YG1H1.

35   "Trump."

36–37   "'Our House Is on Fire': Greta Thunberg, 16, Urges Leaders to Act on Climate," *Guardian* (US edition), January 25, 2020, https://www.theguardian.com/environment/2019/jan/25/our-house-is-on-fire-greta-thunberg16-urges-leaders-to-act-on-climate.

37   Joseph Guzman, "Greta Thunberg Hits Back after Treasury Secretary Mnuchin Tells Her to Study Economics," Hill, January 23, 2020, https://thehill.com/changing-america/sustainability/climate-change/479586-thunberg-hits-back-after-mnuchin-says-she.

38   Guzman.

39   David Wallace-Wells, "It's Greta's World," Intelligencer, September 17, 2019, https://nymag.com/intelligencer/2019/09/greta-thunberg-climate-change-movement.html.

SELECTED BIBLIOGRAPHY

Alter, Charlotte, Suyin Haynes, and Justin Worland. "*Time* 2019 Person of the Year: Greta Thunberg." *Time*, December 4, 2019. https://time .com/person-of-the-year-2019-greta-thunberg/.

Emanuel, Kerry. *What We Know about Climate Change.* Cambridge, MA: MIT Press, 2018.

Gessen, Masha. "The Fifteen-Year-Old Climate Activist Who Is Demanding a New Kind of Politics." *New Yorker*, October 2, 2018. https://www.newyorker.com/news/our-columnists/the-fifteen-year -old-climate-activist-who-is-demanding-a-new-kind-of-politics.

"School Strike for Climate: Meet 15-Year-Old Activist Greta Thunberg, Who Inspired a Global Movement." *Democracy Now!* December 11, 2018. https://www.democracynow.org/2018/12/11/meet_the_15_year _old_swedish.

Shepherd, Briana. "Greta Thunberg's *La Vagabonde* Voyage Let an Aussie Family Meet the Girl behind a Climate Movement." ABC.net.au, December 5, 2019. https://www.abc.net.au/news/2019-12-05/the-real -greta-thunberg-emerged-aboard-la-vagabonde/11766208.

Watts, Jonathan. "Greta Thunberg, Schoolgirl Climate Change Warrior: 'Some People Can Let Things Go. I Can't.'" *Guardian* (US edition), March 11, 2019. https://www.theguardian.com/world/2019/mar/11 /greta-thunberg-schoolgirl-climate-change-warrior-some-people-can -let-things-go-i-cant.

FURTHER READING

Books

Onuoha, Chinwe. *Climate Change and Life on Earth.* Minneapolis: Lerner Publications, 2019.

Shoals, James. *What Is Climate Change?* Broomall, PA: Mason Crest, 2020.

Sjonger, Rebecca. *Taking Action to Help the Environment.* New York: Crabtree, 2020.

Websites

Fridays for Future
    https://www.fridaysforfuture.org/

NASA Climate Kids: What Is Climate Change?
    https://climatekids.nasa.gov/climate-change-meaning/

National Geographic Kids: Greta Thunberg
    https://www.natgeokids.com/nz/kids-club/cool-kids/general-kids
    -club/greta-thunberg-facts/

INDEX